UNTETHERED

Deborah L. Staunton

V Press LC
www.vpresslc.com

Consistently committed to publishing
writing that 'Rises Above' as our motto states.

ISBN 979-8-9854670-2-4

PRINTED IN U.S.A.

1361 W. Wade Hampton Blvd.
Suite F, PMB 162
Greer, SC 29650
(864) 334-5909

PRAISE FOR UNTETHERED

"*Untethered* erupts from a deep place of pain and passion in a straightforward, honest exploration of life, loss, and family. Deborah L. Staunton explores the severe realities of her life as a daughter, wife, and mother with a poet's eye. She sees clearly beneath the surface in these heartfelt pages that investigate the meaning of family and familial mental illness. Dare to enter Staunton's world. You will gain insight, empathy and be deeply moved, and, quite possibly, forever changed."

> —Linda Leedy Schneider, LMSW, Author of *Some Days: Poetry of a Psychotherapist*, Editor of *Mentor's Bouquet*, and Founder of the Manhattan Writing Workshop

"Staunton writes with the depth of a life not only well lived, but keenly witnessed, profoundly pondered, and intuitively observed with a poet's eye unafraid to stare into the sinews of reality. These are poem/stories told in an unflinching collage of pain and poignancy, evocative coming of age memories of city streets, suburbia, and of being a daughter who *"took the lead, guid[ing her] parents through thorny thickets, stoic and stable, a repository of reason."* To experience Staunton's unforgettable writing is to invite her heart into yours, her soul to embrace your own, and to allow her words to indelibly imprint themselves in your mind forever."

> —Dorothy Randall Gray, MSW, MDW, Award-Winning Artist, Spoken Word Poet, Former LA Poet-In-Residence, Author of *Soul Between The Lines*, and Executive Director at Heartland Institute for Transformation

"*Untethered* is a book of metaphors: this is this. A mother's body is bedrock. Addiction is a roller coaster, mental illness, a soundtrack. Family trauma, faith, failure are umbilici to the past. The unknown is a train. All of this is a circle, cycling, spiraling, an endless *if-then*, a coiled spring. In her debut collection of poetry and prose, Deborah L. Staunton unwinds the sobering multigenerational facts that fetter the dreams of this life, her life. *Untethered* is a book of grounding and, ultimately, release."

> —Marj Hahne, Editor and Creative Writing Instructor

"In *Untethered*, Deborah L. Staunton's writing gives a clear and balanced look at family struggles, at mental illness and the path it sometimes takes from one generation to another. Her memoir, shaped by prose and poetry, shows the strength and courage it takes to survive her father's alcoholism and mental illness, wrenching pregnancy losses, and then the challenge of raising a bipolar daughter. Her clear eyed descriptions of what must have been nightmarish experiences honor her resilience as a daughter, a woman, and a parent over the course of her family life. *Untethered* powerfully engages the heart, mind and spirit of the reader. These are stories that need to be told."

—Judith Prest, Poet, Artist, Creativity Coach and Author of *After* and *Geography of Loss*

Some names have been changed to protect privacy.

DEDICATED TO

my mother,
Barbara O'Sullivan
for staying when all the others walked away

and to the memories of my grandmother,
Margaret Sternberg

and my best friend,
Rina Miguel Cristy
always in my heart

TABLE OF CONTENTS

UNDERTOW
After Deborah Paredez's "Self-Portrait in the Year of the Dog"

She is surrounded by waves of white satin,
while men in black suits stand, anchored
at her side. The Rabbi's words lead
her into the depths of her future, this
woman who will be my mother, just
a girl of seventeen, making a promise
she believes she can keep, determined
to save the boy by her side, committed
to untying the ropes that bind him, convinced
in all her teenage ardor, that saving him
is within her reach—
this man-boy who will be my father
leans in, searching for a savior.

BORROWED MEMORIES

Moving through the quiet morning light where her daughters slept in the small, winter-chilled living room, my grandmother reached toward the radiator for a pair of children's socks. Lifting the blankets, she slid them, freshly warmed, over tiny waiting feet. The warmth began its gradual climb from leg to knee to belly and chest, settling over the still-sleeping child in a tangible, heat-infused expression of her mother's love.

My own mother's voice captures and holds these images, the textures, and the quiet intensity of this ritual. The telling and re-telling winds its way into my subconscious and wraps into the fiber of my soul. It is my mother's memory; it belongs to her. Yet, in some small but significant way I have claimed it.

This claiming of memories continues with my own young daughter as she asks me to repeat one story she has come to know so well. She knows about the small scar on my head, the one that came from a heavy wooden attic ladder unfolding on my unsuspecting six-year-old skull, my young frightened mother waking me every few hours to check for signs of concussion. She knows that some forty years later, I still cringe with any small reminder of that day. From mother to daughter to granddaughter, our memories bind us, and the act of their imparting creates a bond between the generations. It was the memory of my mother's difficult pregnancy in which she almost lost me that helped me to endure three miscarriages as I struggled to bring my own baby into the world. And, it is the memory of my mother's strength and endurance during my own childhood that fuels my most difficult days as a parent.

Memories of shopping trips with my mom come back to me as she and my daughter make their own. The three of us continue to thrive, to endure, and to love. We do it with borrowed memories.

MAGEN DAVID
After Kate Buckley's "My Mother's Closet"

Dime-sized six-pointed star
encircled in gold, its delicate chain
always around my mother's neck.
Held close to her flesh just below
her throat, like a freckle or a mole,
infused with all her mother held
close—faith, family, lives lost
in the name of Judaism, burned
into her heart, seared
into the fabric of mothering.
A gift for her thirteenth birthday, the year
Jewish children join the tribe.
Pinned to the underside
of her own daughter's
wedding gown,
beneath layers of lace,
I carry this mark
hidden yet not unseen.

UNTETHERED

The train's horn is low and dense like the fog that envelops the street. Standing on my brother's twin bed, I peer into the darkness just above the garage. He once rode a bicycle across its gray-shingled roof, airborne and untethered, releasing the gleaming handlebars, face full of wind. Tonight the air calls to the trees that hover along the back fence, its tenor piercing the train's bass. A dog barks at the crescent moon, a neighbor's screen door creaks, a flash of headlights streaks across the top window pane. Fireflies dance through the darkened leaves blinking like fairy lights woven through the trees.

Pots and pans clank and rattle below, spaghetti sauce bubbles, its oregano scent curls and winds its way up the stairs to mingle with the fresh soap smell of washed sheets. I'm supposed to be asleep. The front door opens, Daddy's keys jingle, footsteps heavy on the stairs, whiskey invading the soap and oregano. His thunderous voice drowns out the train. I wonder if Mom thinks about the roof and dreams about the day when she too will be untethered.

SMOKE

The school bus disappears down Woodhull Avenue. Mom meets me at the screen door. Hot smoke spirals up from the Salem between her fingers. Her lips are ashen, her jaw tight. Why was she home from work so early? Why was she smoking? It's been ten years since I've seen her with a cigarette.

"I need your help."

I glance behind her into the darkness of the house. My feet are leaden, invisible roots winding their way through the hot cement of our front stoop. The door whines when she opens it. I force myself to follow her into the kitchen, always dim under the amber dome that hangs above the table.

Where was Daddy? Did he try to kill himself again? Did he hurt someone? Was he dead?

The house is quiet, too quiet. My ears tingle, straining for a hint of something. Mom sits and pats a chair for me to follow. I lower myself to the chair, my eyes meeting hers. I can see her reluctance. She takes another drag from the Salem, lets it out slowly and touches my hand.

"Daddy's drinking again."

Her cigarette fades into its own smoke and disappears. Somewhere, Daddy's liquor bottle looms.

FLYING

I'm nine when my dad tells my brother and me that he can fly. I think he's joking. People don't fly. But he doesn't flinch.

Later, he lies on the bed, eyes closed, arms at his sides, quiet and still as death. We stand there waiting, holding our breath, watching intently for him to lift up and take off like Peter Pan. Maybe we have to think happy thoughts like Wendy, John, and Michael. If only happy thoughts could replace the unfathomable ones in my dad's mind. Instead we spend eternity in a neverland of delusion.

Daddy doesn't move, not a fraction of an inch. He just lies there for a long time and then he opens his eyes and sits up.

"You didn't fly!" I accuse him. "Why didn't you?"

"I did. Didn't you see?"

Were we supposed to go along with this charade? Pretend that we saw him fly?

"Daddy, I was watching the whole time. You never even moved."

"I did. I levitated off the bed a little. You weren't looking close enough."

Indignant, I yell, "That's not flying! You said you could fly!"

"C'mon Deb, people can't fly around like birds. But I can levitate and that's something."

"Yeah, it's something," I say, head drooping.

It's late spring when I find the newborn bird on the ground near the chimney, naked and lifeless, blue veins visible through translucent skin. Standing there, staring down at it, I wonder if it thought it could fly too. Maybe it was an outsider in the bird world, its differences perceived as weakness. After all, it thought it could fly when clearly it could barely move.

THE DRIVE-IN

I was six when I overheard my father tell my mother that he planned to kill me. It was the middle of the night and I'd awakened from a fitful sleep to the hushed and urgent tones of my parents' voices moving through the darkened house. My father's despondency had permeated our lives, seeping through the walls and into my dreams. That night, as I listened to his frightening words, I thought about the drive-in. It was my only reprieve from the despair that clung to our home like some toxic strain of ivy.

And now, some thirty years later, the paper said the old drive-in would re-open for the summer and I'd left work early for the three-hour drive upstate. It was an unseasonably cool September evening when I handed a twenty to the kid in the booth, took my change, and pulled into the open lot. It had been raining earlier and the ground was still damp. I parked the car and headed toward the playground. Dark clouds filled the evening sky and a group of rowdy teenagers, sprawled on the hood of a car, took a brief break from their roughhousing to leer at me. Large beads of rainwater clung to the deserted playground equipment. I pulled my sweater tightly around my shoulders as an icy wind swept past, pushing a single swing in a forlorn and awkward movement. The slide, a dark, hulking mass in the center, stood silently in the rapidly dying light. Brushing the sleeve of my sweater across the swing, I sat and looked at the empty playground, my thoughts wandering back to that long-ago summer.

I was dressed in my pajamas, the backseat a jumble of blankets and pillows. Mom packed brown paper grocery bags with sandwiches, apples, and strawberry licorice. We paid the man in the little booth, Daddy drove through the gate, and we embarked on a search for the best speaker in the field of talking boxes. Before he could get it securely fastened to the door, I begged to go to the playground, practically tripping over myself to get out of the car. I could see the other pajama-clad kids and hear their shrieks and peals of laughter from the other side of the grounds.

"Go ahead Barbara, take her. I'll meet you there in a minute."

Bursting onto the playground, I could hardly decide where to start. Spying a free swing, I jumped on and sailed upward, the warm summer air pushing my hair out behind me. Pumping my legs, I pushed higher, until the exhilaration of being there joined with the dizzying height of the swing. From up high I could see the slide in the middle of the park. It must have been a million feet tall, a regal structure with the dying sun glinting off its shiny surface. Jumping off the swing, I ran toward it and scrambled up the steps. When I reached the top, my breath caught as I stood there looking out over a perfect world, a ribbon of pink sunlight tying it all together. Perched there, I remained immobile, poised to absorb every minute detail, transfix it in time, and store it away in my mind like an old snapshot. Looking out over the parking lot, I saw my father approach the playground and scan it briefly before spotting us. He came up behind my mom, whispered something in her ear, and she laughed and rolled her eyes.

"Daddy, catch me!"

Sitting with my legs in front of me, I spread my arms out to my sides and flew with a freedom I've never known since. Seconds later I came to an abrupt halt as I met with the firm grasp of my father's strong, safe arms.

The sun was almost completely down as we walked back to the car. I yawned in the warm summer air, mesmerized by the intermittent glow of fireflies.

As we made our way around the snack stand, the pleasant aromas of buttered popcorn, grilled burgers, and cheese pizza followed us back to the car.

Once there, I piled into the back seat and settled in among the bedclothes.

Adjusting the dial on the speaker, Dad said, "It's still fuzzy. We can't watch the movie with fuzzy reception."

Then I heard the sharp crack of a bottle cap.

Mom watched as he lifted the brown glass bottle to his lips and said, "Charlie, is that really necessary?"

"There, that'll do it, clear as a bell," he said, making one last adjustment to the speaker.

Mom glanced at the bottle again and turned her attention to me.

"How about some licorice?"

I took it and suddenly the car filled with music.

"Get ready, Kiddo, your favorite part is coming," Dad said with a wink.

As the enormous movie screen burst with pre-show cartoon color, I slowly nibbled the sweet treat, making it last as long as I possibly could and savoring every delicious moment.

My mouth filled with the memory of the licorice's fruity sweetness as the temperature dropped and darkness fell heavy on the playground. A penetrating coldness crept into my hands from the swing's heavy chain as I recalled my father's solemn pledge on that late November night.

Several weeks later, I woke to the muted sounds of my parents' voices in the kitchen. Making my way to the top of the stairs, I sat with my legs folded under me, straining to hear their words.

"I can't take this anymore, Charlie. You've got to get some help."

"I don't want any help, Barbara. I've tried. I just want it to be over. They should have let me jump."

"Do you have any idea what it was like, in front of all those people, to have to calm you down and talk you into the car? What if they hadn't stopped in time? Did you consider, for one moment, what it would have been like for me to have to scrape your body off the tracks? Did you?"

I had crept down the stairs and stood just around the corner of the kitchen doorway. I could see Mom's profile and Dad's shoes and the sleeve of his overcoat. Mom lifted a cigarette to her lips and lit it. The smoke curled upward toward the heaven my father so desperately wanted to know. I hadn't seen Mom smoke since I was very little.

She took a deep drag and quietly said, "Charlie, how could I explain that to a six-year-old? How do you tell a child that her father was so terribly unhappy that he jumped off a moving train and is never coming back?"

In the silence of that moment, I asked God to help my Daddy, to change his mind.

When my father spoke, his voice cracked and each word was forced and heavy. "I've got that figured out, Barbara. I can't leave her, I can't. I'll take her with me. I'll make sure she goes fast, she won't feel anything, she won't know what happened."

Mom closed her eyes and tears formed at their corners. She sat there for a moment, silent and still. When she opened her eyes, her face had somehow changed. With trembling hands, she reached toward the brown, glass ashtray on the table between them.

"I can't let you do that, I won't. I'll do whatever it takes to keep her safe."

"Barbara, I would never hurt her, you know that. You know how much I love her." He was crying. "That's exactly why I need to take her with me."

Silent tears streamed down my face as I slowly headed back upstairs. At the top of the stairs I turned and went into my parents' bedroom. It was still and silent. Dark shadows sailed across the room as the headlights of passing cars threw silhouettes of oak leaves into odd patterns on the walls. I walked past the bed and into the bathroom. Mom's toothbrush stood alone in its ceramic holder. Dad's lay askew on the edge of the sink. I picked it up and stood it, straight and upright, in the little hole next to Mom's. Then I went to bed. As I was drifting off, I thought about the drive-in.

I don't know how long I'd been sitting on the swing but the movie had already started. On my way back to the car, I winced at the heavy smells emanating from the nearby snack stand.

Opening the car door, I realized I hadn't seen a single firefly. The damp speaker was cold and heavy as I clumsily positioned it on the door. Tuning it in, I heard the Vampire Lestat say, "But what if I could give it back to you? Pluck out the pain and give you another life? And it would be for all time? And sickness and death could never touch you again?"

What if you could? I thought and reached into the brown paper bag at my side for a stick of strawberry licorice.

DERAILED
After W.S. Merwin's "Separation"

Daddy's black suit and white shirt, crisp, neatly buttoned, tucked into his waistband. His tie, black, wide, sharp at its edges. His face, clean-shaven, smelling of Old Spice and toothpaste. His hair, jet-black in loose ringlets. His eyes, sky-blue, dark when (he thinks) nobody can see. Soon, the low-rumbling train whisks him and all the cardboard cut-out fathers away through the dense morning fog.

At night, the front door opens, keys jingling. He returns, tie askew, top buttons undone, toothpaste and Old Spice lost in a haze of whiskey breath. Soon, the train leaves without him and his eyes go dark, stealing the light from my own.

I'M SAD WITH YOU

After Jackleen Holton's "I'm Sad With You"

Don't cry, Daddy,
I can't make you happy
when I'm sad with you.
Whiskey heat pours
from your skin and mixes with
your pungent tears.
It fills my head, drowns my heart,
and makes me sad with you.
Don't assault my ears
with your devastating secrets,
a reverberating drumbeat,
pounding despair through my pores,
swallowing my joy,
forcing me to be sad with you.
Take back your sadness,
roll it up and pack it away.
Hide it in the corner,
cover it with my smile.
I'm sad with you—
at least pretend
to be happy with me.

WAITING
After Joseph Stroud's "Knots"

Waiting for the phone to ring,
the signal of another
weekend visit, waiting
for the car ride to end,
for my father
to get close enough,
with his lurching gate,
glassy eyes, sour
whiskey scent, waiting
for my mother's jaw
to tighten, her eyes
to harden,
for the words spit
between them, waiting
to become the weapon,
unsheathed, naked
in a moonlit parking lot,
waiting to disobey,
to grab his keys,
stuff them deep
in the pocket
of my jeans.

THE DINER

The parking lot is dark and Daddy is drunk. Tonight's meeting place is the local diner. Mom pulls up next to Dad's car and I hold my breath as he comes over to meet us. I know immediately that he is drunk and glancing at my eleven-year-old brother, I begin to catalogue my options.

Mom's jaw tightens, her eyes harden, "Charlie you can't take them like this."

Dad's speech is a burst of slurred ugliness, his words filled with derision. "Don't you tell me what I can or cannot do."

Mom stands there, quietly calculating. She suggests that we all go into the diner for something to eat.

Dad refuses and turns to us. "Kids, get in the car."

My brother starts toward the passenger side door but I grab his arm.

"No Daddy, you're drunk."

"Deb, get in the car. I'm your father. You have to listen to me."

"Not when you're drunk Daddy."

My arm moves swiftly and I snatch the keys out of his hand. His face hardens.

"Give me the keys, Debbie."

"No, I can't do that Daddy."

"I said, give me the keys now!"

I stuff them deep into the pocket of my jeans.

"Let's go get something to eat," Mom tries again, and this time Dad agrees. My brother's small shoulders sag, his eyes glisten as he takes a few tentative steps toward the brightly lit diner. We slide into a booth by a window, a broken family trying to put the pieces back together.

Later, cold hamburgers sit untouched on large white plates. Daddy's words are slurred and angry as he continues the drunken tirade that he began in the parking lot. Mom's attempt to counteract this is a combination of quiet reason and controlled despair. As Dad's tenuous grip falters, their voices rise and pierce the growing silence around us, throwing the blatant, judgmental stares of the other diners into sharp relief.

And then, without warning, "I'll blow your head off with the shotgun!"
I never saw it coming.

He refers to the gun that he used to keep in a locked box behind the headboard in their bedroom, the one he purchased to protect his family from

16

intruders. With this sudden outburst, the diner goes completely quiet. I stare into my plate and when I finally look up, my silent plea for help is met with four pairs of eyes locked on our table, three waitresses and a busboy who attends my school. They whisper to each other and the boy looks at me with a combination of pity and horror.

Eventually, Mom convinces Dad to skip the visitation this week and we get back in the car and head home. Mom tries to reassure us that Daddy won't show up at the house tonight or follow through on his threat, but we pack our bags and spend the night at a friend's house just in case.

Sometime later, days, maybe weeks, I steal into my parents' bedroom and peek behind the headboard of the bed they once shared. Mom must have taken the key because the lock is still intact, but the wood is smashed and the box is empty.

BEAVER KILL

The icy water nips at my thighs as I wade into the mountain stream they call Beaver Kill. My younger brother David and I are convinced that its name comes from the water being so cold it could kill a beaver. At fourteen, I'm vigilant, eyes darting around to seek out the dark figure of my dad on the bank behind me. David splashes past and I allow myself to relax, stretching the time into an hour or maybe two. As my lips begin to tremble and the skin on my arms erupts in small bumps, I return from my respite.

"Time to go kids!"

My father's voice is strange in my ears, different. It sounds the alarm in my no longer innocent head. Something's wrong.

"Are you okay Daddy?" I ask as we make our way to the car.

He opens the car door. "Sure. I'm fine. Get in."

We pull onto the long, open highway and head south toward my grandparents' hundred-year-old country house in the Wurtsboro hills. I feel the car lurch forward and speed up followed by a quick deceleration. It's nothing, I tell myself.

Without warning we are barreling down the road again only to slow down so quickly that I am reminded of the frightening amusement park rides that Daddy talked me into riding last summer. Scooting forward, I lean over the front seat just as the lines in the middle of the road become a blurry, yellow streak. Daddy brakes and weaves and the car simultaneously slows and slides into the oncoming lane.

"Daddy! Please! Watch the road!"

I fight to contain my terror in an effort to make him hear my words.

"I'm okay," he says, "Everything's fine."

"No, it's not," I say with a calm I find somewhere between utter terror and forced maturity. "You need to pull over, now," I order him.

"No, I'm okay. It's fine Deb, really.

"Daddy, do you want to kill your children? Because you will. You'll kill us both if you don't pull over right now. You're drunk."

"Okay, okay, I'll pull over at the next rest stop."

I remain perched over the seat, watching the road, willing the car to stay steady long enough to get us to safety.

We pull off the highway and dad parks in front of an old, run-down building. Scanning the area, I see that there is no one around. No anchor in this turbulent sea. We are alone, the three of us. My thoughts claw their way out through suffocating emotions. I turn to David, a small boy in an ocean of fear and despair, eyes wide and brimming, and remind myself not to get pulled under by the panic in his face.

"It's okay," I tell him. "We'll just have to wait here until Daddy is sober enough to drive. We just need to give it some time."

The sun is beginning its descent behind the mountains in the distance. Dusk envelopes the car. My own fear rises with the setting sun. And then, without warning, Daddy begins to speak. His voice is tight and his words come out like he's trying to hold them back but can't.

"You kids, you don't know how hard it's been. I tried. I really tried but your aunt, she locked me out of the house. My tools were in the garage. They were mine damn it and she had no right, no right to keep them from me. So, yeah, I broke in to get my own Goddamn tools and she called the cops. You kids, you have no idea what it was like."

He's crying, tears flooding his face and dripping off his nose. I silently beg him to stop, to spare us, to let us be kids a little longer.

"They took my clothes and put me in a cell, naked. They didn't even give me a blanket. Locked me up in a dark, empty cell. It was cold. They took my clothes."

"Why did they take your clothes, Daddy?"

"Because they thought...She told them I might…"

"Try to hurt yourself?"

"Yeah, that's what they thought. It was a nightmare. It was such a nightmare."

I am quietly grateful for the people responsible for saving my father's life.

He continues to talk, rambling about injustice and a world filled with terrible people known only as "they." "They" locked me up and "they" treated me like a criminal, "they" didn't care or understand.

Just stop talking, stop crying, let me breathe, let me think.

"It's okay, Daddy. You're not in jail anymore."

I glance at my brother. They are both depending on me. I somehow need to fix this, to fix us, to stitch together the frayed and tattered ends, to fashion a cloak of normalcy around a family as exposed and vulnerable as my dad was in that cell.

It's fully dark now. With the headlights turned off on the empty country road, the night is a vast, black void. Daddy turns the key and the engine rumbles.

"Are you sure you can drive now Daddy?"

19

He's calmer now, composed, a fair resemblance to his sober self.

"I'm fine Deb." His gaze is steady and unwavering, eyes boring into my own. "You trust me, right?"

"Yes, Daddy, I trust you," I say, swallowing hard and willing myself to believe my own words.

I slide back into the seat behind him and silently say a prayer to get us home safely. He starts to back out and turns to face us.

"Kids, listen, this is very important. You absolutely cannot mention any of this to Grandma and Grandpa. Okay? Not one word. Got it? You have to promise."

When we pull up the long, narrow driveway, Daddy can easily pass for sober. Grandma greets us at the door.

"Hi kids! Did you have a good time? Dinner's ready, we've been waiting for you."

I glance at David, a silent agreement to heed our father's plea thick in the air between us. We slide into the picnic table in the glassed-in area of the old kitchen. I've always loved sitting at this table surrounded by large windows overlooking the property. Sometimes in the early morning or just before dark, the yard fills with deer gracefully nibbling the vegetation. Tonight, the windows are black, an impenetrable darkness devoid of stars. There's no moon, not the slightest flicker of light. Grandma serves her favorite dish, pork chops and a steaming bowl of sauerkraut. Her eyes smile as she fills our plates.

"You must have had so much fun! I bet that water was ice cold though."

My grandparents have a small, elderly beagle named Lucky, and David and I have always referred to them as "Lucky Grandma and Grandpa." Tonight, they have no idea how lucky they are. And it has nothing to do with their dog.

RUNAWAY TRAIN
After Joe Wilkins' "Night"

What I remember, what is etched in my mind, is the name of the roller coaster, a whisper, a warning, an omen—Runaway Train. What I remember is Dad's voice, firm, insistent, inflexible. You must do this Deb, just once, but you must. What I remember is climbing in, legs trembling, the clank of the cold, metal bar swinging over our laps, the click when it locks me in. Inescapable. What I remember is a creak from the gears, the slow roll of the train on its track—taunting, just long enough to give hope before lunging fast, speeding up and lunging, lunging, whipping around the track. The crowds on the ground now blue, green, yellow, red streaks. What I remember is pushing my head into Dad's shirt, closing my eyes, spinning around that track in darkness now, willing myself to stay put, starting to stand, to get out, jump, be done. What I remember is Dad pulling me back and the animal in me sinking my teeth into the flesh of his restraining hand. What I remember is the slap of Dad's free hand on my tear-streaked cheek. What I don't remember is the ride slowing down, stopping. Climbing back out, my legs still tremble, my cheek still stings, indignation roils in my gut.

PIZZA

"Daddy should be here in about an hour," Mom says, gathering her coat and purse. I grip the kitchen counter. Turning toward the front door, she says, "Don't stay up too late. I'll see you in the morning."

"Okay."

At the front door, Mom turns back to face me. The one-word response belies my usual talkative self. Daddy hasn't been back to the house since they split up, but tonight Mom has a work event and Daddy is spending the night with us.

"It'll be fine. He's your father. You'll be in your own house. Don't worry."

"Can you call later?"

"I'm sorry, honey. I don't think I'll have access to a phone, but I'll come up and check on you when I get home."

I close the door behind her. David must be up in his room, and Sandy's probably sleeping by the back door. It's David's turn to feed her.

I walk through the silent house. The pristine furniture in the formal dining room is silhouetted in the evening light. Stiff-backed chairs sit in stern consternation around the barely-used table. In the living room, royal-blue upholstery gives off a slight sheen in its recent freedom from the clear plastic covers that imprisoned it during my early childhood. Despite finally having permission to enter these rooms, completely off-limits before Dad left, I continue to walk past them, invisible velvet ropes a perpetual presence in my consciousness.

The family room on the other side of the front door is empty except for dark paneling, orange and rust shag carpet, and a large wall unit housing my parents' record albums; it sits as unused as its formal counterparts. When the house was new, Daddy built sliding wooden doors with fancy spindles and installed them in the two arched openings to close this room off. It has never held a couch or a TV and despite its name, we've never spent a single minute in there as a family. Banned from the family room as well, I often watched TV in my parents' bedroom.

When we moved from the Bronx to this house in the suburbs with its strawberry fields and barbecues, I was three and David was an infant. Mom wanted to raise her children "in the country." She and Dad chose a large colonial as the ideal home for raising a family. Mom baked cupcakes and filled little baskets with treats for my school parties, she was an assistant leader for my Brownie troop, and she made goodie bags for all my friends on my birthday. She cooked elaborate hot meals every night but made sure that David and I were fed and in bed before Dad arrived home from work on the evening train. We hated being sent to bed before the sun went down. We hadn't yet understood that Mom was protecting us.

Daddy always came up later to say good night. When he leaned over to kiss my cheek, I smelled the liquor on his breath. Even then, I knew it brought his sadness to the surface; I knew that I was the salve for wounds that burned his soul, a glimmer in the darkness that shadowed his eyes. I carried that knowledge without question, determined to be whatever he needed me to be.

Tonight I check the clock, sweeping the house for triggers: notes that can be misconstrued, small gifts left by Mom's new man, (we adore him, and he adores us), green bottles of the Rolling Rock beer he prefers. Exhaling, I glance again at the clock.

There's a sharp knock on the door.

Daddy no longer has a key to the home that was his until less than a year ago. I unlock the door and turn the knob. On the front porch, in the yellow glow of the outside light, he is thinner than he was this time last year, his coat hanging loosely on his frame.

"Hi, Daddy."

He steps in and hugs me. "Hi, Deb. It's so good to see you. Where's your brother?"

"He's upstairs. I'll get him."

I run up the steps and tell David that Daddy is here. He puts down the Legos in his hand and follows me downstairs, eyes downcast, thin arms limp at his sides.

In the kitchen, under the familiar light of the lamp hanging over the table, Daddy tells us about the carpentry job he is doing and talks about our cousins, the ones he is living with since he moved in with our aunt and her family. I can't concentrate on what he's saying. Instead, I focus on the set of his jaw, the way he keeps looking around, eyes darting quickly from one thing to another, hands fumbling with his keys. After about thirty minutes, Daddy asks if we want pizza. A rare treat! We are both excited and eagerly tell him yes.

"I'll go pick it up. You kids wait here. I'll be back soon."

He leaves and takes some of the tension with him. David goes back to his Legos, and I put on the TV. Forty-five minutes later, I check the time. He should be back any minute. An hour passes and I go back downstairs to look out the window and down the road, hoping to spot his car. By the two-hour mark, I'm pacing, wishing I could call Mom. Finally, after two and half hours,

Daddy walks in the door with the pizza. His eyes are red and glassy, liquor smell sharp on his breath and clothes. I follow him into the kitchen.

"Pizza's here! Come and get it!"

"Daddy, where were you? You've been gone a long time."

"I wasn't gone that long. Traffic was pretty bad. Come have some pizza."

"Have you been drinking, Daddy?"

"No, no. Like I said, just a lot of traffic."

He puts the pizza on the table, and I get three plates from the cabinet.

Pulling a chair out, he stumbles.

"Daddy!"

"I'm alright. It's okay. Have some pizza."

He grabs a slice from the box, cheese dripping off the end. When he brings it to his mouth, the cheese gets all over his chin. David and I glance at each other, eyes wide.

"Damn," he mumbles. "How could she—"

The phone rings. Daddy lurches across the room and grabs the receiver in a greasy hand.

"He—, hel—, hello?"

After speaking in low tones, he suddenly gets loud enough for me to hear what he's saying. "I love my kids. I really do. I love them so much. Nobody understands."

He's crying now, big heaving sobs, tears running down his cheeks and into his mouth, mixing with cheese and liquor.

"They don't get it. I try so hard. I really do. I tried. You know I tried. I don't know what else to do."

David and I stare at this spectacle, waiting for something, anything, to make it stop. I will Mom to come home, praying that she can sense me. The house looks different, feels different. The faux brick linoleum floor is unsteady beneath my feet. The kitchen seems to tilt like a sinking ship.

Daddy hands me the phone. I put it to my ear.

"Hello?"

"Hi, Sweetie. Listen, your daddy is drunk. You need to get him to lie down. He needs to sleep it off. Okay, Honey?"

Aunt Dianne's voice is soothing, an anchor in this storm.

"Okay. I'll try."

"I want you to call me back when you get him to bed. Can you do that for me?"

"Yes, I can do that."

"Okay, I love you."

"I love you too."

I hang up and take Daddy's hand.

"You need to lie down now, Daddy."

"No. What about the pizza?"

He flings my hand away, grabs the pizza box, and lunges into the foyer, pitching to one side. I snatch the box from him and put it back on the table. Sandy runs between us and barks.

"Come on, Daddy. You need to lie down."

He sways and grabs the wall, pizza grease smearing its snowy surface. I take his hand again and put my arm around his waist. He nods, and we make our way toward the stairs. He leans against me, and I stagger under his weight. Step by step, I drag him to the top of the stairs and into David's room. Sitting him on the bed, I pull off his shoes, lift his legs and cover him with a blanket. He is asleep almost instantly, pizza grease gathering in the corners of his mouth.

I exhale, close the door behind me, and go downstairs to call Aunt Dianne.

"He's sleeping now. I put him to bed. I took his shoes off."

"I am so proud of you, Debbie. You're a brave, strong girl. He'll sleep it off and when he wakes up, he'll be better. Where's Mommy? Will she be home soon?"

"She's at a work meeting. I don't know when she'll be home. Thank you, Aunt Dianne."

"It's okay, Honey."

I hang up the phone. David hasn't said a word since Daddy got back with the pizza.

"It's okay now. Daddy's sleeping, and Mommy will be home soon. Its okay."

He nods and we spend the next couple of hours in separate rooms. Just before midnight, Mom gets home.

"You're still up? It's late. Is David asleep?"

"I don't know, Mom. It's been a rough night."

"Why? What happened?"

I start to tell her. Her face falls and her eyes glisten.

THE PATHS WE TAKE

The train grumbles toward the platform, straining as it slows, gears grind, it calls out its arrival, a painful shriek of metal against metal. My father's eyes, unfocused, register only the dirt-streaked window and nothing beyond. He is blind to the businessmen in rumpled suits, weary and sluggish from their long commute. Stained and flattened coffee cups evade his gaze. Even the shine of discarded chewing gum wrappers fail to ignite a spark.

When the train begins to move again, he stands and makes his way to the end of the car. Pushing the door open, he slips into the space between the cars and watches as the ground blurs beneath him.

Then he jumps.

The train's speed is minimal and my dad's body lands and rolls down a grassy embankment. He is physically unhurt but this failed and feeble attempt at suicide will haunt his family in ways he will never know.

I am thirteen when my oldest childhood friend casually mentions it, oblivious to the fact that I am unaware. The only working mother in our early '70's neighborhood, my mom fields suicide calls and begs him to wait until she can get home. She manages to talk him out of taking his own life numerous times until his threats encompass a frightening new element. He tells her that he can't stand the thought of being without me and that he's going to "take me with him," because he loves me too much to face death alone.

By some odd combination of fate and my mother's tenacity, my father manages to avoid suicide until, at age forty, leukemia claims his life. Decades later I find myself questioning fate and my own perseverance when my twelve-year-old daughter threatens to kill herself.

PHONE CALLS

"Debalah, come. Talk to your Aunt Dianne," my grandmother calls in her thick
Hungarian accent, its familiar cadence comforting.

Taking the heavy, yellow receiver from her hand, I put it to my ear.
"Daddy's in heaven now." The words echo in my head before they are spoken.
My body sags in relief. It's over. There will never be another moment of dread,
another heart-wrenching unburdening of my father's emotional turmoil on my
16-year-old psyche, no more breath-holding anticipation of the next episode, no
more wondering if this will be the day it ends.

There will be no more hugs or quiet talks, no more pride in my
accomplishments, no more unspoken understanding of a social awkwardness
we shared. I don't have a dad anymore. My mom is a single parent.

Despite the brutal nature of the divorce, they will always be connected
through their youthful union and the two children they share. We are three now
instead of four.

And now I am faced with the task of having to tell my mom that my dad is
dead.

My mind travels back a few months to a visit with family friends in their
upstate New York home. Mom was visibly upset, unusual for her as she always
kept a composed and quiet strength in the face of adversity. When she refused
to share the cause of her distress, I intuitively spoke the words on my mind.
"You're worried about when Daddy dies aren't you?" Her face registered
surprise and caution at the same time. "You don't know how you will get
David and me through it, how you will handle the grief for all three of us."

"But how...?"

"You're our mom and you want to take our pain away, but we are going to
lose our dad and you can't stop that or control it. You can't grieve for us. All
we can do is grieve together. David and I need to feel our own feelings. You
can't make that go away. We'll be okay"

And now, at the moment that I so confidently assured my mom would be
alright, I am paralyzed with the reality of it. We are alone, each of us in a
different corner of the country, one of us on Long Island, one in Florida, and
me here in the Bronx. "We have to call Mom," I tell my grandmother, but the
mere thought of making that phone call destroys me. She picks up the phone
and dials. The blaze within me flickers and goes out in the face of the flame I
am about to witness. I hear my grandmother's words, "Barbara, Charlie died."

And now I reach for the phone, eager to hear my mom's voice, to connect with my one remaining parent.

"Mommy?"

"Hi Sweetie. It's going to be okay. We just need to be strong until we can be together again. Take care of your brother. I will see you as soon as I can."

"Will I see you before the funeral?"

"No, Honey, I won't be at the funeral. His family, well, they told me not to come," I squeeze my eyes tight together.

My mother continues, "I'm not welcome there, and I don't want to cause any drama."

"You won't be at the funeral? We have to go alone?"

The next day, Gloria arrives. She is my best friend's mom and as close to a mother as I have in the absence of my own. She sits on my grandmother's worn beige sofa and puts her arms around me. Then, in her exceedingly gentle voice, she tells me that my brother and I will be traveling to New Jersey to sit Shiva, the traditional Jewish mourning ritual, with my father's family.

"What? No. No I'm not going. I won't."

"I know you don't want to go, and I understand how hard this is for you," she whispers, "but you have to go. You have to honor his memory and do the right thing. It's family."

Growing up, I spent much of my childhood in this woman's home. I was a part of her warm, loving, Filipino family and I understood the importance of family and respect. I nod and gather my resolve one last time.

VOYAGE

I am the daughter who surrendered her childhood to her father's anguished tears, whose wisdom arrived on a derailed train, draped in a liquor-drenched coat, dragging a suitcase of delusions wrapped in cellophane. Lessons learned through the looking glass of convoluted conversations, I am the daughter who took the lead, guided her parents through thorny thickets, stoic and stable, a repository of reason. I am the daughter who sees her father's darkness echoed in the shadow of her daughter's eyes.

MOTHER LOVE

From warm womb
to golden-lit bedroom,
canopied crib near
soft, draped bed.
From one life to another
bedroom to bedroom,
white lace cradle
perched by my own mother-bed.
New life
completing the circle,
soft, amber glow
on breasts taut
with mother's milk
that feeds my soul.

BEFORE YOU LEFT
After Ross Gay's "Poem to My Child, If Ever You Shall Be"

Before the blood soaked through the sheet
of my dreams.
Before the cramps took hold.
Before the drumbeat of your heart
ceased its rhythmic thumping in the distance.
Before the silence filled my womb.

Your song pulsed,
Your fingers tapped our rhythm,
You arrived before you left,
thread yourself into my consciousness,
Your breath tightened my chest,
rendered me sleepless,
Your distant cries pierced my waiting ears,
Your bird-like mouth, an open call to my empty breasts.

Before you left, you arrived.
You slipped in, weaved yourself
through the fabric of my mind,
claimed your rightful place.
You were here
before you weren't.
Your shadow looms
above the thin sheet,
spreads across it
and hovers, light as air
on my heavy heart.

HOLDING ON

Tiny kidney-bean shape
motionless on the ultrasound screen,
infinitesimal heart
stilled by a hand
much greater than mine;
the silent waters of my womb
within a static, gray vessel
devoid of the life
so recently there;
my own thundering heart-beat
gallops forward
refuses to stop pumping
the blood and nutrients
needed to sustain the life
it has housed
for such a brief moment;
the life-force that beckons
to every mother
to fiercely protect her unborn
refuses to loosen its grip
on my creation;
I hold tight
to the tiny life
I had no hand
in *un*-creating.

MOVEMENT

her lips form a strained line
body motionless
                              just like my unborn baby.
            I will her

to move, just a flick of a finger,
a drop of a shoulder,
or a barely discernible breath,
                              one small sign

from the tiny silhouette on the screen,
the gift of movement,
                              any movement.

the technician stands
                  mannequin still,

refuses to make eye contact,
                  to release the breath

we're both holding.
in the tight confines of the room,
                              time twists into eternity.

if she would just speak
just say the words,

                  break the silence

and make it stop.

            my baby may be dead,
but I'm not.

WE NAMED HIM JONAH

Unlike the first two, the third one crept up, gray and hovering. There were no jolts of hot pain, or passing of blood and tissue, no waves of fear and nausea, no minuscule fetus forced from my body in a twisted version of labor and delivery. Instead, there was stillness, a dark bean-shaped smudge in the center of a screen, a cavernous silence where the whoosh and tick of a heartbeat once was.

For ten days this baby stayed with me in the warmth and darkness of my womb, no outward sign, not a whisper of distress.

"Are you okay? There's something different in your face."

How do you answer when your body is so full of emptiness?

Like a tooth extraction or an appendectomy, a D&C is a "simple, medical procedure," Except that it's not simple, and it's far more than a medical procedure. I know what to expect, having been here only fourteen months earlier. I recognize the medicinal smell, the buzzes and the beeps of the monitors, the dull, colorless walls, the familiar jargon.

Naked, except for the faded blue hospital gown, I shiver and the nurse drapes a heavy, heated blanket over me. She struggles to start an I.V. and resorts to using the back of my hand. I cringe and look away.

"You have such tiny veins," she says, "and tiny, little hands too."

I nod and try not to think of the tiny hands and feet of the baby who refuses to leave the warmth of my body on his own.

The ambulatory surgery wing is two floors below the maternity ward, two floors separating high-risk pregnancies and multiple miscarriages from the lusty cries of healthy newborns.

When they wheel me into the freezing O.R. everything around me is eclipsed by the blinding white light of the enormous fixture directly above me. The anesthesiologist is at my head, his voice a steady drone in my ear and then a second later a nurse is calling my name. Like my pregnancy, the D&C seems to be over before it began. Tender and groggy, I am on my way home less than three hours after I arrive.

I return to work two days later and move through my tasks with sluggish determination. A weight blankets everything, making a pencil or a coffee mug an effort to lift.

When the large manila envelope arrives in the mail, I open it with trembling hands. My doctor already informed me of the lab results, but the visual confirmation is harrowing. I study the strange, caterpillar-like marks of the karyotype. Their story written in a single word: abnormal. Searching the unfamiliar image for the intangible, I will the black symbols to rearrange themselves into something less foreign, less removed from the son I'll never know. Trisomy 13, the least common and the most severe of the viable trisomies. We name him Jonah.

The second piece of mail is a standard white envelope from my insurance company. The numerous doctor and hospital charges are all covered, except for one. The anesthesia fee is listed in full under "patient responsibility." Assuming it's a mistake, I dial the customer service number.

"Thank you for holding Ma'am. The billing statement is correct. We don't cover anesthesia for abortions." He's young, a kid. I struggle to control the bile rising in my throat.

"I didn't have an abortion. It was a miscarriage."

"Well, Ma'am, the computer says you had an abortion, and we don't pay for abortions."

"It wasn't an abortion! It was my third miscarriage! We wanted this baby so much." Hyperventilating, tears streaming, all attempts to remain composed are gone while the kid stays steady, almost mechanical.

"Ma'am, it is coded as a spontaneous abortion. As I told you before, we don't pay for abortions."

I'm screaming now. "Spontaneous abortion is the medical term for miscarriage!"

"I'm sorry Ma'am, we don't pay for abortions"

The paper in my hand is rattling, adding to my own violent cacophony. I hang up and slide down the wall until I'm curled and crumpled on the floor. Abortion. The word assaults me, cutting, slicing, taking my only solace. If only money could wipe this away. But paying the bill will not erase the accusation, the belief that my baby was not wanted, that his death was a choice. I look down at the statement in my hand and two words scream back at me. St. Charles. An abortion was never even a possibility. It was a Catholic hospital.

AMNIOTIC WASTELAND

After Kaveh Akbar's "Portrait of the Alcoholic Floating in Space with Severed Umbilicus"

Legs clamped in stirrups,
lower belly buried
in viscous gel, womanhood
invaded by this reed-like
ultrasound wand, zygotic runes
carved onto static gray screen.
Minuscule fetus, fossilized,
its hieroglyphics imprinted
on dusty uterine wall, embossed
with embryonic remnants,
prelude to a deep curettage
of amniotic wasteland.

SEEDS

The small, potted plant, a condolence gift from co-workers, sits on a windowsill, sunlight dancing on its tiny, green leaves. I've never been able to grow plants. Their leaves shrivel and turn brown, their stems go brittle and bare. Like my womb that refuses to sustain the tiny seed so recently planted there, this plant will die too. One morning its brown-tipped leaves will droop and in a blink it will stand lifeless in its small pot in front of a rain-streaked window. Plants and babies: tender things that defy the heart, slipping away before they take root.

Except that this plant stubbornly refuses to die. For days, then weeks, then months it grows, blooms, thrives. Hope returns at its quiet insistence. It brings with it a steady heartbeat, soft tentative kicks against my rounding belly. The plant keeps pace with my pregnancy—full, green, healthy. When I bring my newborn daughter home on a warm, spring day, sage green vines wind their way down the front of her little white gown in tiny, precise stitches.

Sunlight welcomes us with its warm embrace as I glance at the plant on the windowsill. Its leaves are beginning to brown.

WHAT ALMOST WAS

When being pregnant and not being pregnant melted together. When, multihued, it slid into my consciousness and out again, a goldfish, a shimmering flash of iridescent scales visible long enough to glimpse before disappearing into the watery shadows. When you poured love and hot tea.

When our second miscarriage crashed into me, fiery like a lightning bolt, an unexpected jolt in the velvety blackness. When every gristly detail stood in sharp relief. When you caught and released my tears with your own.

When our third baby remained in the shelter of my cave-like womb, still, lifeless, like an old clock, hands frozen in their circular trip. When you wrapped yourself around me and held my breath with yours.

When baby number four, a semi-colon suspended on a sonogram screen, bobbed like a buoy in barren waters.

When you held our daughter as she buried her head in my chest and cried for the siblings she never knew. When we grieved for a future that almost was.

LIFE BLOOD

A woman's blood volume doubles during pregnancy. Her heart works twice as hard, pumping liquid life through the cord that binds her to her unborn child. But a few crimson drops reveal themselves and her heart thunders a fierce response to this ominous sign.

While pregnant with me, my own mother hemorrhaged. Confined to bed, she invoked a second cord, a ribbon of prayer gently binding my tiny heart to her own, willing it to continue beating, weaving the ends of that ribbon around something greater than both of us. I answered her call, my unremitting movement the perpetual drumbeat of our mutual dialogue.

Decades later I summon her strength as that same life blood carries four unborn babies from my body. And once again, when finally pregnant with my son, he squeezes the umbilical cord, cutting off his own oxygen.

Despite this, he moves, little feet marching out their rhythm, tiny fists pummeling the cave-like walls of my womb. When he arrives, they lift him into the light, no longer dependent on the blood coursing through the cord.

Our bodies instinctively curl toward each other, his legs moving in their perpetual dance. His mouth opens and roots for my breast, searching for that other nourishing liquid. My body continues to sustain him, as his languid eyes beckon me closer to the thin veil that separates the world he so recently left from the one we now share.

BETWEEN LOVE AND MADNESS

The vibration of my cell phone is a hot coil
in my head. It travels down my neck, shoulders, arms, settles
in my chest, filling my lungs with a pneumonia of dread.
I silently beg the Gods of Motherhood
to let this one be minor.
With each event my own mental health falters
and threatens to join my daughter in this dangerous dance.
I know the steps by heart,
lessons learned at a tender age by my father's side.
The music of mental illness is the song of my life,
genetics the cruel composer,
chance the foolish gambler.
I was the lucky one.
I escaped its prison,
yet I remain in its grip,
between my father and my daughter.

THE MOMENT THAT EVERYTHING CHANGED

"She's shy," I say when my three-year-old daughter's pre-school friend greets her with a friendly, "Hi Sadie!"

Sadie looks away then turns her head into my arm.

Later, at the post office, a woman in line in front of us makes eye contact and smiles. "How old are you sweetie?"

"She's three," I answer automatically, knowing that Sadie won't respond.

I tell myself not to be concerned. She's only three. Some kids take a while to warm up.

During the next two years, she remains silent when anyone other than family addresses her. She's been speaking in complete sentences since she was eighteen months old and is extremely verbal and communicative at home. She tells stories, has a great sense of humor, and sings constantly. She chats happily with my husband and me, our parents, and even my best friend and her son, but she hasn't said a single word to my brother who adores her. It is a world that remains a mystery to us as we try to understand the dichotomy that is our daughter.

Her kindergarten teachers suggest testing and a few weeks later, "shy" becomes "selective mutism."

Sadie is classified for special education services and the school begins to address her rather unusual diagnosis. Now I whisper, "She has selective mutism," when strangers are friendly.

I desperately want to say, She's not being rude, it's just that... But I can't provide a long-winded explanation to everyone who receives a blank stare in response to a question or friendly hello. The world of selective mutism becomes our normal. Still difficult, embarrassing, and frustrating. But it's our normal just the same.

During the next two years, Sadie has weekly sessions with a therapist, participates in a social skills group, and is eventually prescribed an anti-anxiety medication. And very slowly, she begins to talk. It is unpredictable and sporadic, but she gradually moves forward.

And then one day in second grade, she asks if she can join the chorus at school. She walks around the house singing all the new songs she is learning, and my stomach tightens at the thought of the upcoming concert. Will she sing? Will she freeze?

Bouncing off the school bus a few weeks before the concert, she says, "Mommy, I auditioned for a solo!"

A what?!!

"That's great, honey, I can't wait to hear it."

And three weeks later, on a stage in front of a packed auditorium, my selectively mute daughter steps up to the mic and sings. Her voice, sweet and melodic, flows into the hushed room like a stream in a quiet wood. As the tears run down my face, I look around at the other parents, their faces flushed with pride in the dim glow of the room and wonder if anyone else knows that this is the moment that everything changed.

THE KNIFE

"Mama, wake up, wake up Mama!" The bright September sun cuts through the room from the skylights above the bed.

"Ok Honey, just a few more minutes. Mama's tired."

"Mama if you don't get up by the time I count to ten, I'll get a knife and cut you."

The sleep instantly retreats. Clear-eyed and focused, I report for duty immediately. But she is already gone, her defiant little steps echoing across the cold kitchen tiles. I blink and she's back, standing in the doorway gripping a steak knife in the same hand that created the rainbows and butterflies that hang on the fridge in the same kitchen that houses the knife now gleaming in the morning light of my bedroom.

I inhale slowly and listen to the voice in my head, the voice of my own mother, the voice of the self I am still becoming familiar with. I swallow hard over the un-nameable emotion in my throat and stride with false confidence toward my daughter and the knife. My arm moves swiftly as I snatch it from her small hand. Her grip loosens, her jaw slackens, she surrenders.

"Go get ready for school now," I tell her.

She obeys, the damage is done, her need temporarily sated. She sings as she zips up her backpack, a little girl getting ready for school like any other. I watch her through wary eyes, questioning everything I've ever known.

And later she watches me through the small, rectangular window on the bus, peering out with something akin to satisfaction tinged with regret. I am grateful for the respite as the bus lumbers down the street carrying my child into someone else's consciousness. But even respite has a price. Heading back into the empty house I prepare myself.

Sadie has been seeing a therapist for almost three years. The first one was funny and down-to-earth, and she assured me that there was no need for concern. Sadie was just headstrong and stubborn. My instinct told me otherwise, and a stack of colorful business cards in my pediatrician's office led us to therapist number two. If therapist number one was not serious enough, therapist number two proved to be too grave in her assessment of Sadie's issues. Almost every session included the grim words, "She's a very ill girl." In addition to the weekly reminders that my daughter was very ill, there came advice, each time I reported something positive, not to get my hopes up because it wouldn't last. The support and encouragement I so desperately needed was conspicuously absent. Instead, I internalized her negativity and approached each interaction with her with a pervasive sense of anxiety. Today is no exception.

In an effort to push through this difficult task, I decide to call her immediately. I dial the number and attempt to keep my shame at bay. The therapist's voice immediately weakens my façade. My own voice falters as I repeat the mantra she has taught me in rare moments of encouragement: "Always trust your own intuition. Remember that you know your child best. Don't doubt yourself." She is all professionalism, any trace of camaraderie a faded memory.

"You need to take her to the psych ward today."

I blanche. "She did it for a reaction" I tell her. "I'm certain of it." Sadie's behavior was often extreme and unusual. This morning's outburst wasn't the first time she threatened violence. In a moment of frustration she once told me, "I will kill myself and Sam, and then you will have no children." But this morning was different. She had never before followed a verbal threat with a physical one.

"You need to take her to the hospital," she repeats without hesitation.

"But I know my child best," her own words form my desperate plea. "Are you saying you know more than the experts?" she asks.

I harbor no doubt that Sadie's "threat" was a brilliant attempt to draw something from me, to fill a void that I perhaps created, but it was in no way an actual intention. Of this I am certain.

"No, but I know my child best," I say less convincingly. My own insecurity prevents me from giving in to my anger and frustration, and I swallow the desire to confront her with the hypocrisy of the question she has just thrown at me.

"If you don't take her, I will have to call Child Protective Services." The tenuous thread between us snaps. She informs me that she will be calling Sadie's psychiatrist, a doctor we only recently started seeing when we made the hard decision to medicate her.

I wait for Dom to get home from work so that we can take Sadie to the hospital together. We tell her that she needs to see a doctor because she threatened to hurt me. It is a concept that a six-year-old can't fully grasp, but she seems satisfied with the explanation. On the way to the hospital my cell phone rings. Alerted by her therapist, Sadie's psychiatrist has no words of comfort or support. She simply says, "You have two choices. Take her to the ER or check her into South Oaks, the local psychiatric hospital." I inform her that we are on our way to the psychiatric ER and hang up. My natural instinct to respect authority fades with the sound of her voice. I can no longer trust this person with the well-being of my family.

The familiar pediatric E.R., a place of empathy and concern, no longer brings the sense of relief I felt upon entering its doors with a feverish infant. The long, cold hallway leading to the psych ward is quiet and spare, the nurse solemn and efficient, her plain, gray scrubs a stark contrast to the colorful, teddy bear-themed ones worn by the bubbly nurses in the "regular" children's E.R. She stops at the end of the hall and three large men with short haircuts and muscled biceps emerge from a door on our right. Sadie clings to my leg. Dom takes my hand. One of the men asks, "Is this the six-year-old?" The nurse nods and the men, like a pack of pit bulls, step forward in one slow, deliberate move. Sadie's grip on my leg tightens, her bravado stolen by "hospital protocol." The men try to engage but she pushes her face into my thigh, willing them away and triggering every mothering instinct I ever had. Their massive hands gently peel her miniature ones from my body, guiding her toward the door. When she looks up, her eyes, like a Margaret Keane painting, singe my soul.

A meaty arm points to a door across the hall and a male voice says, "Go in there," the only words we'll hear for the next two hours. The room is a small, rectangular windowless box with built-in benches along the walls. We sit in near silence, the image of those three hulking men with my tiny girl, a continuous loop playing in my mind like an old, silent movie.

When an older woman opens the door and beckons us to follow her, it is nearly 10 p.m. A young male psychiatrist and female social worker greet us with smiles in a well-lit office. Relieved, I immediately sense that we are no longer "suspects" and proceed with complete transparency, eager to be heard. As Dom and I catalogue the day's events along with all pertinent psychological and behavioral history—Sadie's diagnoses of generalized anxiety disorder, selective mutism, and possible mood disorder—it becomes apparent that they not only understand but agree with our perception of the situation. Their smiles and nods appear genuine, and when the social worker asks, "So she says and does things for shock value?" I know that she understands my daughter better in the brief time she has known her than Sadie's therapist does after two years of therapy. Ten minutes later they bring Sadie out and tell us that we are free to return home. She is neither a threat to herself nor to anyone else.

Sadie bounces into the hallway with her shoes in her hands. She appears completely unfazed by the evening's experience and oblivious to the trauma it has caused us. "Mommy, they gave me pizza and let me play video games. Oh yeah, and they took my shoes. Let's go home now."

"Yeah Sadie, let's go home."

The following day when her therapist calls, I am eager to share the validation I finally received at the end of an incredibly long night.

"We were there for hours," I tell her. "They evaluated her and spoke with us and concluded that she posed no threat. They sent us home."

The smile drains out of my voice when she says, "You know, the only reason they didn't admit her is because they didn't have enough beds." And then, as if to affirm her own assertion, she adds, "She's a very ill girl."

VOLCANO
After Sarah Kay's "Dragons"

At four years old she charges in,
bull-like and ferocious.
At six, steely-eyed and stubborn,
she plants her feet
in obstinate determination.
By nine, an inferno of pent-up rage
explodes in violent threats,
raining down on me
in molten showers.
This child, detonated
by the slightest injustice, erupts
with soul fury, eyes blazing, small
body rigid with indignation.

SCISSORS

My cell phone rings and I answer quietly, trying not to disturb my co-workers. I've come to expect the regular calls from Sadie's teachers this year. She's refusing to do her classwork, she's rolling her eyes, she's proffering a blank, vacant stare in response to any request that makes her uncomfortable.

I brace myself.

But today's call is not from her teachers. The school psychologist apologizes for interrupting me at work. Sadie needs to be picked up immediately. She's brandishing a pair of scissors and needs to see a doctor. When her teachers removed all of her books and art supplies from her desk in an attempt to get her to focus on the lesson, Sadie managed to grab a pair of scissors and is behaving as if she's going to hurt herself.

I grab my purse and keys. "I'm on my way,"

When I arrive, Sadie is alone, lying on the carpet, scissors in hand. Her teachers and the psychologist inform me that they didn't take the scissors from her out of fear that she would become aggressive. She's nine years old, has never been physically aggressive at school and four adults combined couldn't manage to get a pair of child's scissors away from her.

I squat down by her head and whisper, "Come on Sadie, get up."

She does, and uncurling her hand, I take the scissors from her. Assuring the staff that I will take her directly to the E.R., we walk out of the building together.

Sadie is silent and I follow her lead, taking the opportunity to formulate my thoughts. She sits in the back seat, gazing out the window and then asks, "Where are we going?"

"To the hospital,"

"But why? I wasn't going to hurt anyone. Mom, you know I wouldn't hurt anyone."

"I know Sadie but your behavior said otherwise and nobody at school knew what you would do."

Having been to the psych ward before, I contact my husband Dom, and prepare myself for the long night ahead of us. This time we wait for eight hours. Once again, they release her with no concerns for her safety or the safety of others. I tuck the paperwork into my bag.

The on-going drama of this year has usurped any sense of normalcy that we might have had. I don't doubt that there will be another incident, just wonder when to expect the inevitable.

Two months pass before the phone signals another emergency. Sadie locked herself in the closet and is refusing to come out. I leave work and rush to the school again. When I get there, Sadie is sitting at her desk in the empty classroom. She is suspended for the rest of the day. It is clear that her teachers, though well meaning, are unable to handle the situation. Their helplessness fuels my own. I am fully supportive of any efforts they make, but suspending a nine-year-old for hiding in a closet forces me to question their ability to provide my daughter with what she needs.

As we leave the building, Sadie's silent scowl persuades me to wait until we get home to talk with her. Later, she yells at me, "You knew it was picture re-take day and you didn't send my pictures in! You embarrassed me!"

Sadie, I forgot. I didn't do it intentionally."

"Yes you did! I hate you!"

"What were you doing in the closet?"

"Writing in my diary."

"Why didn't you talk to the teacher? She would've helped."

"I don't want her help. You should've sent the pictures in."

"I'm sorry Sadie. I meant to but it slipped my mind. You need to find a better way to deal with your feelings."

"Mom, I was so embarrassed. I couldn't come out of the closet. I just couldn't."

"Sadie's teachers and the special education program in our district have been incredible since Kindergarten. The school part of the equation was working well while the home component took five years, four therapists and two psychiatrists to ease the chaos of our daily life; until now, when fourth grade is proving to be the year that the school puzzle piece refuses to fit with the rest of the picture. The boundaries are less clear. Sadie's mental illness is no longer confined to our home. There is no respite. One day blends into the next, broken only by fiery outbursts disrupting the deceptive façade of a false calm.

TO THE WOMAN WHO STOPPED HER CAR TO SCREAM AT ME AT THE BUS STOP

May you never know the heartache
of mothering a mentally ill child,
the breath-stopping anticipation of the next phone call,
the debilitating exhaustion
of fending off her demons—your own,
suicide threats,
a rope around the soft flesh of her young neck,
eight hours in the psychiatric E.R.

May you never feel the helplessness
of watching your five-year-old refuse to eat
and fail to grow,
tiny ribs sharp against paper-thin skin,
begging him to take just one bite,
scales and growth charts
mocking with menacing numbers,
the specter of a feeding tube
haunting your sleep.

May you never find yourself caught
between two impossible choices,
a demanding boss
and the child in need
of all you have.

May you never wake
day after day
with knots of uncertainty gnawing your gut,
not knowing
not wanting to know.

May you never be on the receiving end
of the scorn you so easily dispense
blissfully unaware

of battles waging all around you.

THE BITE

Our bodies are twisted in a jumble of limbs, hair, and torsos, one tiny, one large. "Don't do this," I say through gritted teeth as her elbow hits me in the ribs and her feet pummel my belly like an enraged fetus. "Come on Sadie, put your shoes on, we're running late."

"No!"

Grabbing a small foot, I bring her shoe toward it with my other hand. She yanks it away and kicks me in the face. Panting and full of rage, I lunge for her ankle and clamp down with my teeth. She screams in shock and pain and I am suddenly and completely deflated.

Sitting there on the playroom floor, rocking my five-year-old in my arms amidst a flood of our combined tears, I hear an eerily calm and deliberate voice. You just bit your child. Denial is no longer an option. There's no going back now. No amount of wanting or wishing or hoping will change what has just become so painfully clear.

Grabbing her backpack, I check on my sleeping son. Buckled snuggly into his stroller, he is blissfully unaware of this morning's scene. A severe case of laryngitis has also kept the volume to a one-sided din. We can still make the school bus if we hurry.

There is no house on the corner lot where Sadie gets on the bus. I park the stroller on the grass and use my foot to lock the brakes. Sam is still asleep. From the corner of my eye, I see a blur of color as Sadie dashes up the short street behind us. Knowing that the large hill up ahead will completely block her from view, I tear after her, heart pounding as a car approaches. I reach her just as the car crests the hill and yank her off the street as it speeds past us. Panting and shaken, my reprimands are no more than whispers from my swollen larynx. I take her hand and we run back down the road to the still sleeping baby as another car slows to a stop on the main cross-road in front of us. A middle-aged woman with a boy of about twelve in the passenger seat starts screaming.

"How dare you leave a baby! What's wrong with you? A baby in a stroller!"

With the sting of this unexpected assault, I forget that I have no voice, and fighting tears, I squeak out, "My daughter was in the street. I had to get her."

The woman barks back, "So you take the stroller with you! How dare you leave a baby!" Then she demands, "Are you their mother?!"

Defeated, I nod and she pulls away just as the school bus arrives.

DISCIPLINE
After Martha Collins' "Witness"

If she says something now
I'll yell something hateful.

If I yell something hateful, she'll call me a monster. If she calls me a monster, it
will make itself bigger—bigger than me, bigger than her, bigger than us. If she
calls me a monster it will wound with the truth.

If I say something now,
she will feed off my words,
she will feed off my soul,
devour me whole.

If I say something now, I will shatter the calm, I will shatter myself, my child,
my world. If I say something now, she will scream something too. If she
screams something too, I will give it right back, I will lose what I have, I will
need what I've lost. If I need what I've lost, she will need what is gone.

If she needs what is gone,
I won't have it to give.

SHOES

Sadie is at the end of the aisle in the back of the shoe store, sprawled on the floor, refusing to remove the high-heeled shoes I won't buy for her. I stand with my four-year-old at the other end of the aisle, holding the boxes containing the sneakers and sandals we came in for.

The saleswoman gives me a knowing smile. "I'll take care of it," she says with a confidence I envy as she strides toward my daughter while I stand there feeling helpless. When she returns she has the shoes in her hand. I pay for the ones in my own and turn toward the aisle from which my daughter is still refusing to leave. It is 5:00 p.m. and the culmination of a day spent ignoring, cajoling, threatening, reasoning, yelling and probably at some point, begging. In the past four years, I have consulted with developmental pediatricians, neuropsychologists, teachers, therapists and psychiatrists. Sadie's diagnoses are incomplete, the professionals are not quite sure what is going on and they have been unable to provide me with the tools I need to address our situation and bring order to the chaos. I inhale, breathing deeply and use a calm yet authoritative voice.

"Sadie, it's time to go."

"No!"

Pushing back the urge to indulge my weary mind and heavy heart with the anger and frustration I've come to know too well, I begin to catalogue the "helpful advice" and "non-judgmental opinions" that are so easily offered up by the well-intentioned. I make a decision based on nothing more than the knowledge that I haven't used this approach before and the novelty alone may prove successful this time.

"I'm just going to pull my car up to the front," I say to the woman, trying to assure myself as much as her that I am not about to abandon my child. When Sadie sees me heading for the door, she jumps up.

"I'm not going," she says.

"Then I'll have to call the police," the saleswoman responds.

Sadie's face registers this threat and she obediently follows me out of the store as I give the woman a quick thank you with my eyes.

But it's not over yet. In fact, it has just begun. Sadie refuses to get into the car. Instead, she climbs up onto the roof and perches there like a defiant squirrel on a shaky tree limb. Knowing that a confrontational approach will undoubtedly backfire, I buckle my son into his car seat, get behind the wheel and spend the next twenty minutes silently enduring the stares and whispers of the many people passing by—the people who don't know that Sadie has been in therapy since she was four and on meds since she was six, the people who don't know that my own sense of failure is far worse than the blame or disapproval of a stranger, the people who don't know that there is more to this story, and more than one way to tell it.

THE CONFESSION

It's dusk and the homework battle has been fought but not won. There are no winners in the struggle of hearts and minds and fierce emotion. There is only an end, abrupt and harsh or gradual and drawn out. Tonight's drama was brief and thankfully not too intense.

Afterward, I sit in the living room, weary and waiting for the clock to give me permission to put an end to another draining day. Soon, soon they will sleep and so will I. But not too soon. I'm not ready to do it all again. Tonight, though, it is not meant to be. Tonight there is another hurdle, one that I cannot prepare for or anticipate.

Sadie runs from her room in a burst of 9-year old energy, hyperventilating, her face a veil of fear.

"Mommy, mommy when I came back from the bathroom my window was open and my mattress was all cut up!"

"What? Wait. What?"

"Really Mommy, my window is open and my mattress is cut up."

Part of me, the part that knows too well the motivations of my troubled daughter, pauses just long enough to make a decision.

"Get your shoes, let's go," I tell the kids as I usher them out of the house and into the car.

"Sadie, you need to tell me the truth."

"I am Mommy. I promise."

Pulling into a nearby parking lot, I grab my cell phone, begin to dial and stop. My gut is telling me to get real. I can't call the police until I know for sure. Instead, I call my husband, Dom, at work. He tells me he'll come home, to go to a friend's place and wait.

Later, Sadie crawls behind me in the big living room chair, our close friends waiting and watching. I turn and meet her wide, hazel eyes with my own dark ones.

"Sadie, you need to tell me the truth. I really mean it."

Her face registers the seriousness in my voice.

"You did it, didn't you?"

Tears well, she looks down and in a small voice, she says, "Yes."

Just yes.

I immediately call Dom and tell him to stay put. When I hang up, Sadie is curled in a corner of the couch and my friend and her husband are speaking with her in firm, yet gentle tones. They remind her of the consequences of her choices.

"Daddy almost left work. Mommy almost called the police. You frightened your little brother."

They tell her how much she is loved, how many people care about her, including themselves. I silently acknowledge how much I love them for being the village, for stepping in so naturally and for partnering with me when I so desperately need them.

The small, sad figure on the couch belies her usual angry, defensive self. I hold my breath and my tongue, fully expecting a rage-filled outburst, accusations, maybe even threats. Instead, she nods, apologizes and listens, truly listens.

BIPOLAR DISORDER

After Peggy Shumaker's "Asthma."

The reason she wouldn't tell the waiter what she wanted. The reason Mrs. T took the scissors from her desk. The reason sleep slipped passed us night after night. The reason I screamed when I should have whispered. The reason her friends were forced to find the good. The reason others couldn't. The reason homework battles were hostile and locked doors were dangerous. The reason her raging was relentless and solace was out of reach. The reason suicide threats and psych wards invited my own unraveling. The reason knives knew stories no one wanted to write. The reason we held our breath when breathing was unbearable. The reason feelings were feathers, caught and tossed on the wind. The reason her father and I fought and feared, and grew apart. The reason I shouldered the shame. The reason I still do.

THE MAN IN THE SHED

As I unlock the front door, the kids push each other, each one trying to get inside before the other. My five-year-old manages to squeeze his small body through before Sadie and she relents, having won the earlier battle over which door Sam could use to get out of the car—she has forbidden him to get out on 'her' side.

It is 7:30 p.m. and having started my day at 5, I am ready to call it a night. Catching my breath before getting Sam ready for bed, I sink into the couch. Two minutes later Sadie comes in with a look on her face that puts me on high alert. "What now?" I ask myself.

"Mom, I just saw something."

"What did you see?" I ask, not really wanting to know.

"I saw a man in the shed."

Experience has taught me to question my ten-year-old's perceptions if not her honesty.

"What do you mean you saw a man in the shed?"

"He was in the shed. I saw him through the back door."

I get up and walk over to the sliding glass doors and immediately see that the shed door is wide open. Neither kid has been out there all day and the door sticks so much that my husband, Dom, needs a hammer to pry it open.

"What did he look like?" I ask her.

"He was bald with a tattoo on his head and black pants."

"Where did he go?"

"He ran that way," she says pointing toward the neighbor's yard.

"O.K. we need to call the police."

I check that all the doors are locked and then dial 9-1-1. When the police arrive, I let them in, wishing that Dom was here and praying that Sadie is telling the truth. Having a stranger poking around in my shed while I'm home alone with two young children is somehow less upsetting than involving the police in a false report by a ten-year-old.

Sadie is quiet and serious. She answers their questions without hesitation, his height, his clothing etc.

The officer tells us he is going to wait in his car for the K-9's to arrive. When he leaves I call Dom at work. I need to make him a part of this whether he is physically here or not. When I hang up, Sadie is pale and pacing.

"Mom I need to tell you something."

"What Sadie? What do you need to tell me?"

"I'm scared to tell you."

"You have to Sadie. This is very important.'

"I know but I'm scared to tell you."

"Did you lie? Talk to me."

"I don't know. I don't know if I lied. I don't know what I saw."

"Sadie, the police are here. They are bringing dogs There are going to be men and dogs out there in the cold looking for a man that doesn't exist."

"I know. I'm sorry"

"Why did you do it?'

"I don't know. Mommy, I have a big ball of guilt in my stomach."

Something in that plaintive admission is unusually reassuring. She feels guilt, she has a conscience, and she's finally willing and able to express those feelings verbally.

When the officer returns I am fully prepared to thank him for his time and end this embarrassing charade. Instead he tells me that the dogs picked up a scent that does not belong to anyone in my family. My mind immediately jumps back to this afternoon and the open shed door. Coincidence? Perhaps. Despite my fear, I am secretly relieved

BROKEN

At times my soul is shattered.
The longing for a lost dream,
the letting go of the fairy tale,
the harsh, penetrating knowledge
that it will never be, never has been, was never meant to be.
At times like these, I lose myself in a sea of unforgiving demands,
the waves of failure rising up to dizzying heights,
pausing only for seconds before the inevitable crash,
leaving me breathless and soaked,
shivering and pleading with the fates to turn the tide.

My anger recedes with the water,
slowly moving out to sea
only to return for the next storm.
Until then, I breathe deeply of the salt air
and resolve to fight harder next time by not fighting at all.
I berate myself for failing her, for failing myself, for failing us
for struggling again and again and again,
for allowing my child's demons to cripple me,
for not being strong enough, capable enough, good enough
at times like these
to fix her, to fix us, to fix this.

A PHILOSOPHY OF FRACTURE

Through

No breaking of waters, just a fine, thin slicing, the splitting of skin. This child, who broke ground after three failed pregnancies, who painted the world crimson, spurned the muted pastels of babyhood, tiny fists punching the air.

Out

At two, at four, at six, she struggled to break out–out of arms, out of laps, out of doors. She blazed on, said she'd kill Sam and herself to make me childless, carved into her bedroom door *fuck* and *shit*, cut up her mattress with a knife she snuck from the kitchen.

In

At fourteen she breaks in–busted window, broken glass, police patrolling. Shattered, we parent in pieces.

Down

Like the window, cracks grow, reach, spread from my center, splinter outward across the surface, ignite every nerve-ending from heart to fingertips, lodge in my core. Fractured.

WHAT I KNOW
After Sharon Olds' "Looking At Them Sleep"

I know a daughter who
sulks in the passenger seat,
head bowed,
musky Mary Jane
invading the space between us.

I know smoky eye shadow
and the crimson lips
of a mouth that once
hungered for my milk.

I know jagged elbows
and long limbs
that turn away,
lanky arms and round breasts
that turn toward another.

I know the silence
of a teenage marijuana haze,
where I once knew
the chirp of childhood.

I know the glow
of a cell phone screen
that pulls her in,
the one-word answers,
the grimace and the flinch
that beg me to fade
into the background.

BATTLEGROUND
After Kayla Kay's "Homecoming"

She is blind, sees only the enemy
created by her own mind,
continues to fire round after round
into the darkness that surrounds
us, barks orders to the rank and file
of her own imagination, gathers ammunition,
stands guard, weapons
at the ready, war cries
piercing the smoky air, a barrage
of gunfire raining down on
a battlefield of adolescent rage. I emerge,
step into the line of fire, peer un-
blinking into the eyes of her lost
babyhood, silently
beg for a flicker of recognition
and quietly mouth the words, "It's Mommy,
baby, put the gun down."

MAYBE SOMEDAY

Maybe someday she will consign
her somber contemplation of blood-
tinged wrists to yesterday's pages.

Maybe someday she will point
her camera in a new direction and frame
her world in unfiltered clarity.

Maybe someday she will navigate
a future of her own design and rewrite
the wreckage of our history.

Maybe someday she will walk through
a sun-lit sanctuary, a white organza veil
replacing the one that hangs between us now.

Maybe someday she will turn
the kaleidoscope of our shared memories
toward a light that fractures the darkness

Maybe someday she will emerge
                              untethered.

IF YOU NEED HELP—MENTAL ILLNESS

Mental Illness affects not only those who suffer from it, but those who live with them and love them. Locating and establishing a relationship with the right mental health professionals is quite challenging and can be exhausting, but it can also make a tremendous difference in the lives of everyone who is affected by mental illness. Keep looking. Keep exploring new approaches. Most importantly, keep talking about it.

Removing the stigma of mental health conditions and care will pave the way to better solutions, healthier families, and more loving relationships.

—Deborah L. Staunton

Below are some resources if you or someone you love is suffering from mental illness:

- Substance Abuse and Mental Health Services Administration (SAMHSA): National Helpline at 1-800-662-HELP (4357).
- National Suicide Prevention Lifeline: 800-273-8255

IF YOU NEED HELP—MISCARRIAGE

One in four women suffer pregnancy loss. That's 25% of all women who will lose a pregnancy*. Although the number is large, the stigma is larger. Miscarriage is rarely talked about. Often, women who suffer a loss feel so isolated in their experience that they tell very few people and believe that they must carry on as if nothing happened. If women lose a child during pregnancy they are not given the grace that they are given if they lose a full-term or living child. For women who suffer multiple miscarriages, the woman is often questioned about what she might have done to cause the loss. During this grief, often endured alone, this type of questioning can be devastating. Like with mental illness, we need to remove the stigma, we need to talk about miscarriage, we need to educate those around us on the need for support and understanding.

—Deborah L. Staunton

Below are a few resources available for miscarriage support:

- American Pregnancy Association
    - Getting-Pregnant
    - Pregnancy Loss
    - Genetic Disorders & Birth Defects
    - After a Miscarriage: Surviving Emotionally
    - Symptoms & Signs of a Miscarriage
    - Chemical Pregnancy
    - D & C After a Miscarriage
- March of Dimes:
    - Wall of Remembrance
    - Type 'Miscarriage' into their search bar.
- World Health Organization
    - Follow this path: Home/ Newsroom/ Spotlight/ Why we need to talk about losing a baby**

---

* Greves, Christine, C., MD, "Pregnancy Loss: 1 in 4." *Orlando Health: Winnie Palmer Hospital for Women and Babies* October 30, 2018. https://www.winniepalmerhospital.com/content-hub/pregnancy-loss-1-in-4.
** https://www.who.int/news-room/spotlight/why-we-need-to-talk-about-losing-a-baby

LITERARY ACKNOWLEDGMENTS

Much appreciation is extended to the editors of the following journals in whose pages these works first appeared:

AROHO's *Waves Anthology*: "Movement"
Bards Annual: "Derailed"
Bold + Italic Magazine: Mother Love"
Dragonfly Magazine: "Flying"
Literary Mama: "To the Woman Who Stopped Her Car to Scream at Me at the Bus Stop"
Meat for Tea: "The Drive-In"
Mom Egg Review: "Shoes"
Mothers Always Write: "Borrowed Memories"
Pretty Owl Poetry: "Untethered"
Quillkeepers Press Rearing in the Rearview: "Volcano" & "Maybe Someday" & "Waiting"
Running With Water: "We Named Him Jonah," "Undertow," "Before You Left," "Seeds," & "Bipolar Disorder."
Six Hens: "The Knife"
Sparks of Calliope: "Between Love & Madness"
Still Standing Magazine: "Holding On"
The Phoenix Soul: "The Moment That Everything Changed"
The Remembered Arts Journal: "Broken"

SPECIAL THANKS

I'd like to thank my publisher, Torie Amarie Dale, for believing in my work and for giving me the opportunity to achieve my dream, Leehu Sigler, for his wonderful insight and editorial feedback, and Mary-Faith Martinez for taking the time to help fine tune the final copy. Thank you to Chelsey Clammer for formatting my manuscript numerous times with minimal notice and for editorial support and feedback.

This project would not have been possible without Marj Hahne whose time, expertise, love, and passion for guiding poets to be the best they can be, gave me the skill, confidence, and joy needed to make this happen. And great appreciation is given to Linda Leedy Schneider who gave me a safe place to explore poetry before I had ever written my first poem and who encouraged me to believe in the poet within me before I knew there was one. I am grateful to Dorothy Randall Gray for bringing warmth and ardor to her workshops and for embracing me in her circle of fierce, beautiful women.

Thank you to Judith Prest and Suzi Banks Baum for giving me the permission and the encouragement needed to create art with joy instead of judgment. With gratitude to Lisa St. John for stepping in to help on a tight deadline with support and compassion. And to Susan Tiberghien for teaching me to listen to my dreams as well as my inner voice—thank you for the wisdom you imparted to me.

No thank you page would be complete without acknowledging the extraordinary support I received from Leslie Neustadt, Catharina Coenen, Heather Summerhayes Cariou, Paula Chaffee Scardamalia, Judy Huge, Maureen Murdock, Joy Ross Davis, Janice Gary, Jan Phillips, Dixie King, Kelly Dumar, Hope Player, and all the women of the International Women's Writing Guild for everything you do for women writers and for the guidance, the sisterhood, and the opportunity that the Guild provides. It is truly a gift.

Thank you to my dear friends Cynthia Armstrong, Doug Kaplan, Sam Cristy, Ellen Kaspar, Debbie Swanson, Sue Knutsen, Frank and April Fazio, Sandy and Anthony Alcide, Gloria and Art Miguel, Linda Brown, and Laura Smith and to my Aunt Rita, Uncle Phil, Aunt Dianne, and Uncle Rob for your love and support. With tremendous love and gratitude to my parents, Barbara and Rory O'Sullivan, for being the constants in my life and for loving, guiding, and supporting me always. Thank you to my brother David for sharing my childhood and for being the best brother anyone could have.

Last, but certainly not least, I am deeply thankful to my husband, Dominic, for 22 years of love, support and friendship, and for taking this beautiful and difficult journey with me.

ABOUT THE AUTHOR

Deborah L. Staunton holds degrees in Early Childhood Education and Theatre Arts. She has worked as an early intervention specialist for United Cerebral Palsy's Parent Infant Program and has extensive experience in the technical aspects of theatre including stage management and lighting for both adult and children's productions.

Deborah's writing has appeared internationally in several magazines and journals, including *The New York Times, Pretty Owl Poetry, Six Hens, Gallery & Studio Arts Journal, The Remembered Arts Journal, Literary Mama, Sheepshead Review, The MacGuffin,* and she has written child development materials for Harcourt Learning Direct.

In addition to being nominated for a Best of the Net writing prize and two Pushcart Prize nominations, Deborah's work has won or placed in several writing contests including First Place for Memoir in The Fiction Writer's Journey, Mother's Milk Books Writing Prize, Writer's Advice Scintillating Starts, Writer's Advice Flash Contest, and Springfield Writer's Guild writing contest.

Deborah is a proud member of the International Women's Writing Guild and continues to write prose and poems to remove the stigma of mental illness. She makes a comfortable home with her husband and a series of twos: two children, two rabbits, and two cats.

CPSIA information can be obtained
at www.ICGtesting.com
Printed in the USA
JSHW011710020723
44053JS00004B/190

9 798985 467024